DISCARDED

Aboriginal Legends of Canada

Mi'kmaq

Megan Cuthbert

Weigl

Public Library
Incorporated 1862
Barrie, Ontario

Published by Weigl Educational Publishers Limited
6325 10th Street SE
Calgary, Alberta T2H 2Z9
Website: www.weigl.ca

Copyright ©2015 Weigl Educational Publishers Limited

All rights reserved. No part of this publication may be reproduced, stored in a retrieval system, or transmitted in any form or by any means, electronic, mechanical, photocopying, recording, or otherwise, without the prior written permission of the publisher.

Library and Archives Canada Cataloguing in Publication
Cuthbert, Megan, 1984-, author
        Mi'kmaq / Megan Cuthbert.
 (Aboriginal legends of Canada)
Issued in print and electronic formats.
ISBN 978-1-77071-301-7 (bound).--ISBN 978-1-77071-302-4 (pbk.).--
ISBN 978-1-77071-303-1 (ebook)
        1. Micmac Indians--Folklore. I. Title.
E99.M6C88 2013   j398.2089'97343   C2013-907326-4
                                                 C2013-907327-2

Printed in the United States of America in North Mankato, Minnesota
1 2 3 4 5 6 7 8 9 0 18 17 16 15 14

062014
WEP301113

Editor: Heather Kissock
Design: Mandy Christiansen
Illustrator: Martha Jablonski-Jones

Photo Credits
Weigl acknowledges Getty Images and Alamy as its primary image suppliers for this title.

We acknowledge the financial support of the Government of Canada through the Canada Book Fund for our publishing activities.

CONTENTS

Meet the Mi'kmaq

The Mi'kmaq are one of Canada's **Aboriginal** groups. They have lived in eastern Canada for more than 10,000 years. In the past, the Mi'kmaq were hunter-gatherers. They hunted, fished, and gathered berries and plants. Today, there are at least 20,000 Mi'kmaq living throughout Canada. Most are found in the provinces of Nova Scotia, New Brunswick, Prince Edward Island, Newfoundland and Labrador, and Quebec.

Storytelling has always played an important role in Mi'kmaq life. In the past, the Mi'kmaq did not have a written language. They used storytelling as a way to share information and entertain one another. Today, the Mi'kmaq continue to use storytelling to pass on their history and **traditions**.

Stories of Creation

Some of the Mi'kmaq's oldest **legends** tell stories of creation. A creation story explains how people believe Earth and everything on it came to be. The Mi'kmaq believe that the Creator was responsible for making the Sun and Earth.

The Mi'kmaq's Mid-Winter Feast is held in honour of the Creator every January during the new moon. During this feast, the Mi'kmaq offer thanks to the Creator through stories and dances.

The Sun circles Earth each day. It brings light and warmth. It also helps the Creator by watching over Earth's people. The creation story tells of a time when the Sun saw people not showing respect for each other. This made the Sun sad. How the Sun reacted to their behaviour set a new course for the people of Earth.

In one Mi'kmaq legend, the Sun transforms a rock into an old woman.

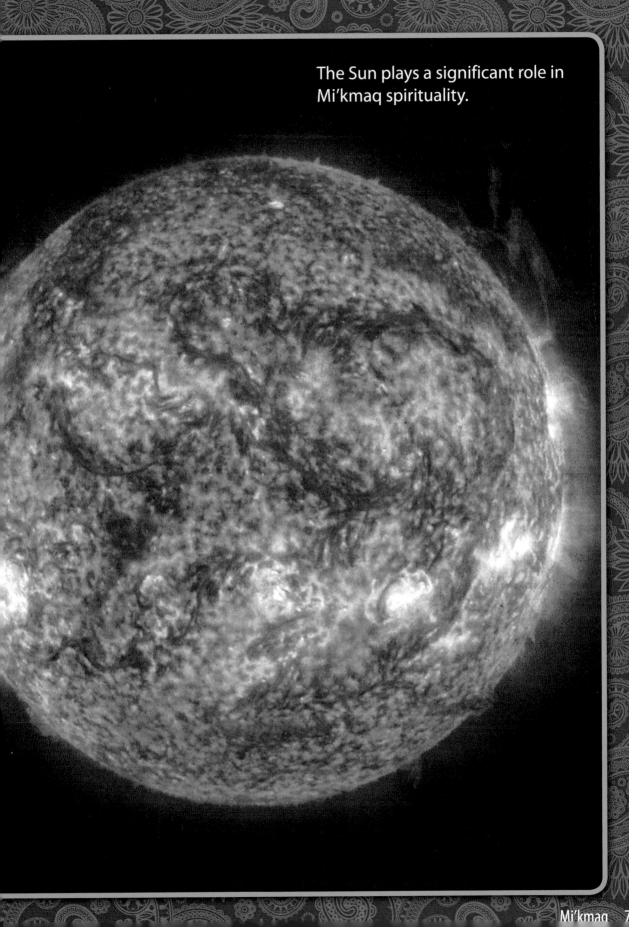

The Sun plays a significant role in Mi'kmaq spirituality.

Creation STORY

Many years ago, the Creator made the Sun as its first born. For a long time, the Sun was alone in the universe. This changed when the Creator made Earth.

The Sun watched over Earth. It divided Earth into many parts and separated them with great lakes. Then, the Sun created a man and a woman to live on the land. The couple lived long lives and had many children. However, over time, the people proved themselves to be angry and mean. Fights broke out among them.

This made the Sun sad. It began to weep. The Sun's tears fell from the skies and covered Earth with water. So many tears fell that Earth began to flood. To escape the flood, the people got into birchbark canoes. However, a wind overturned the canoes, throwing everyone into the water. Only the old man and old woman survived. They were the kindest of all people, and the Creator blessed them with more children. Earth soon filled with people again.

Nature Stories

The Mi'kmaq have several stories that explain the **natural world**. Some of these stories describe how different landforms came to be. Others explain why animals look or behave in a certain way. Many of these stories are told with humour, but have a serious message.

How Rabbit Received His Long Ears tells the story of Rabbit and how he decides to have some fun at the expense of the other animals. When his fun creates problems, Rabbit finds himself in trouble with Glooscap, a caring Mi'kmaq spirit. Glooscap teaches Rabbit a lesson he will never forget.

The Mi'kmaq honour nature and animals. They sometimes carve animal shapes into everyday objects, such as pipes.

The rabbit is often portrayed as a trickster in Mi'kmaq stories.

HOW RABBIT Received His LONG EARS

When he was first put on Earth, Rabbit had short ears. One day, Rabbit was bored. He decided to play a trick on the other animals. Rabbit told Beaver that the Sun was not going to rise again. Beaver became worried and told the other animals.

Soon, every animal was in a panic. Without the Sun, it would be like winter all the time. The animals began to gather food to prepare for the loss of the Sun.

Glooscap saw the animals behaving strangely. He asked them what was wrong. The animals explained that the Sun was not going to rise again. Glooscap knew this was not true. He asked the animals who had told them this. He became very angry when he learned it was Rabbit. When Glooscap found Rabbit, he pulled Rabbit up by his ears. Rabbit's ears have been long ever since.

Life Lessons

The Mi'kmaq use storytelling to teach their children about important beliefs. These beliefs include how people should behave and treat each other. Adults and **elders** want to create fun ways for the children to learn important life lessons. Stories can be told **orally**, with music, and also through dance.

arly Mi'kmaq used rock drawings s a way to communicate with thers. Stone or metal was used to arve into rock surfaces. Many of hese drawings told stories.

The Mi'kmaq admire people who display certain **traits**. They believe people should be kind and help each other. These traits have helped the Mi'kmaq survive during tough times. *The Creator Visits* tells of a young man and his grandfather who receive a visit from the Creator. In the story, the Creator tests the men to see if they are kind and giving.

The Mi'kmaq often beat a drum to signify the beginning of a story.

Dancing is a way for the Mi'kmaq to tell stories and entertain each other.

The CREATOR VISITS

A young man lived with his grandfather in the woods. They were very poor. One night, they both dreamed that the Creator came to visit them. The two men believed it was a sign. They prepared a feast for the Creator's visit.

The next day, two hungry children knocked on the door. The men shared with them the food they had prepared for the Creator's visit. Later, a young man knocked. He was also very hungry, so the men shared their food with him as well. Next, a middle-aged man knocked. He, too, was cold and hungry. There was little food left, but the men gave him what they could. Finally, an old man came to the door asking for food. The young man and his grandfather gave the old man the last of the feast they had prepared for the Creator.

That night, the Creator returned in their dreams. He told them he had visited them four times. As they had shown kindness and given each visitor food, the Creator promised that the men would never be hungry again.

Heroic Tales

Many Mi'kmaq stories feature heroes and heroines. These people exhibit traits that the Mi'kmaq admire. Often, the people in these stories go on long journeys or overcome difficult obstacles. These tales teach Mi'kmaq children about the importance of **perseverance**, courage, and wisdom.

In *The Kidnapping of Glooscap's Family*, an evil sorcerer takes Glooscap's family away. Glooscap is faced with many challenges as he tries to prove that he can keep his family safe. He must rely on his strength and wisdom to rescue them.

The Mi'kmaq believe that Glooscap created many of the landforms found in eastern Canada, including the Annapolis Valley.

Mi'kmaq legend says that Glooscap was created when a lightning bolt hit the sand.

The Kidnapping of GLOOSCAP'S Family

Many years ago, an evil sorcerer named Winpe moved onto Glooscap's land. He was determined to destroy Glooscap. One day, when Glooscap was away from his lodge, Winpe kidnapped Glooscap's family and took them away on a canoe. When Glooscap discovered what happened, he set off after them.

Winpe sent witches and other evil creatures to stop Glooscap. However, Glooscap was wise and used his powers to defeat them. After a long journey filled with many obstacles, Glooscap found Winpe's camp. When Winpe saw Glooscap, he prepared for battle. Winpe called on his powers and grew until his head was higher than the tallest tree. Glooscap also grew. He grew even higher than Winpe, until his head was in the clouds. Winpe saw that he could not win the battle against Glooscap. He surrendered and set Glooscap's family free.

Activity

Make a Porcupine Quill Bracelet

Storytelling is just one way that the Mi'kmaq express themselves. They are also known for making jewellery from beads and porcupine quills. Follow the instructions below to make your own Mi'kmaq-style bracelet.

You will need:

Beads

String, wool, or leather

Safety scissors

1. Cut a piece of string, wool, or leather about 50 centimetres long.

2. Thread the beads onto the string one at a time. You can arrange them in a pattern, or make your bracelet unique by choosing random beads.

3. Continue threading beads onto the string until the bracelet is long enough to fit around your wrist.

4. Thread both ends of the string together through one bead.

5. Tie the strings together with a double knot. Trim the ends with safety scissors. Your new bracelet is now ready to wear.

Further Research

Many books and websites provide information on Aboriginal legends. To learn more about this topic, borrow books from the library, or search the internet.

Books

Most libraries have computers that connect to a database for researching information. If you input a key word, you will be provided with a list of books in the library that contain information on that topic. Nonfiction books are arranged numerically, using their call number. Fiction books are organized alphabetically by the author's last name.

Websites

For more information about Mi'kmaq history and culture, visit:
www.collectionscanada.gc.ca/settlement/kids/021013-2091-e.html

Discover more about the legend of Glooscap at:
www.glooscapheritagecentre.com

Key Words

Aboriginal: the First Nations, Inuit, and Métis of Canada

elders: the wise people of a community

legends: stories that have been passed down from generation to generation

natural world: relating to things that have not been made by people

orally: by spoken word

perseverance: to stick to a purpose or aim

traditions: established practices and beliefs

traits: qualities or characteristics

Index